SUPER SMART THINKING

PSYCHOLOGY MADE EASY

Enslow PUBLISHING

Written by
Jean-Marc Lawton

Published in 2027 by Enslow Publishing, LLC
2544 Clinton Street
Buffalo, NY 14224

First published in Great Britain in 2021 by Wayland

Editor: John Hort
Design and illustration: Collaborate Ltd

Printed in China

CPSIA compliance information: Batch #QS27ENS: For further information contact Enslow Publishing LLC, New York, New York at 1-800-398-2504.

Please visit our website, www.enslowpublishing.com. For a free color catalog of all our high-quality books, call toll free 1-800-398-2504 or fax 1-877-980-4454.

Cataloging-in-Publication Data

Names: Lawton, Jean-Marc.
Title: Psychology made easy / by Jean-Marc Lawton.
Description: Buffalo, NY : Enslow Publishing, 2027. | Series: Super smart thinking | Includes glossary and index.
Identifiers: ISBN 9781978549203 (pbk.) | ISBN 9781978549210 (library bound) | ISBN 9781978549227 (ebook)
Subjects: LCSH: Psychology--Juvenile literature.
Classification: LCC BF149.5 L39 2027 | DDC 155.4--dc23

Find us on

CONTENTS

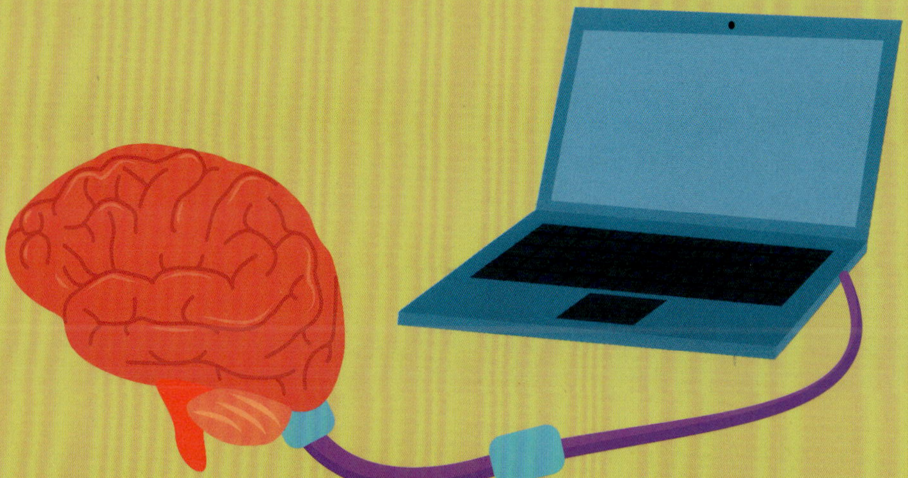

WELCOME TO PSYCHOLOGY

Psychology is the scientific study of the **mind** and **behavior**. But what is your mind? Is it something physical created from your brain or something non-physical like a soul or spirit? And is behavior a product of your mind?

These are basic questions that psychology seeks to answer.

Ψ

The symbol for psychology comes from the letter Psi, which is in the Greek alphabet.

PHILOSOPHY

Psychology emerged out of an earlier subject called philosophy, which studies existence and reality by asking questions such as whether we're born good or not.

In a way, psychology can be seen as a kind of scientific type of philosophy, as psychology applies scientific research methods and principles to the study of human nature.

IS PSYCHOLOGY A SCIENCE?

Psychology is regarded as a science and uses scientific methods, just like physics, chemistry, and biology. However, there are parts of psychology that are non-scientific, and some psychologists believe the mind and behavior cannot be understood through science alone.

This issue will be discussed further in this book.

Psychology is made up of several approaches, and psychology can only be truly understood by considering all these approaches. Each of these approaches will be explored in this book.

PRACTICAL APPLICATIONS

The beauty of psychology is that it can provide useful practical applications that benefit people, such as mental health therapies and relationship counseling, to name but two.

THE BIOLOGICAL APPROACH: IT'S IN YOUR GENES

The biological approach sees the mind and behavior as being products of your physical body, with genes, evolution, biochemistry, and brain structures especially important. Biological psychologists therefore believe a thorough knowledge of biological systems, such as those on this page, can provide an understanding of thoughts and behavior.

GENES, made up of DNA (right), are inherited from your parents and carry information that help form physical characteristics, as well as your mental and behavioral abilities, such as having good language skills.

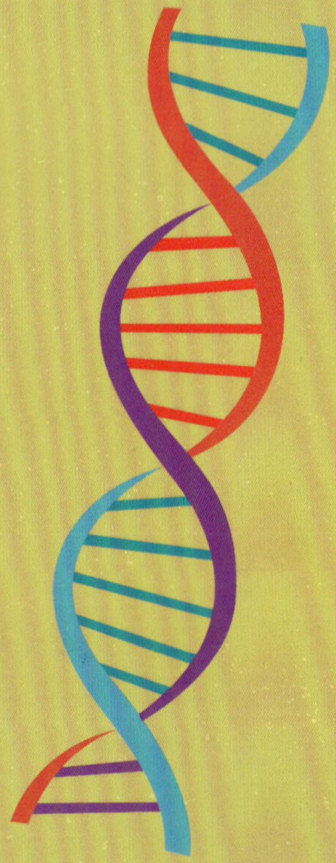

BIOCHEMISTRY involves hormones and neurotransmitters, which are chemical substances that carry messages around the brain and body to influence behavior. For example, the hormone testosterone is associated with aggressive behavior.

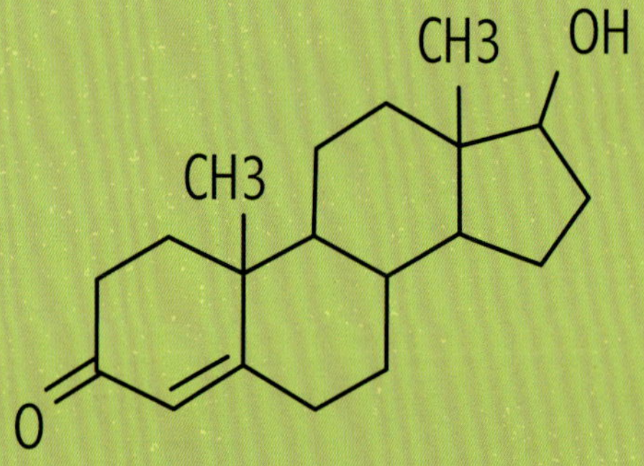

Testosterone (above) is a hormone that is made up of 19 carbon atoms, 29 hydrogen atoms, and 2 oxygen atoms.

EVOLUTION concerns the process of gradual changes, over generations, through the preference for genes that increase chances of survival (natural selection). For example, genes that increase levels of intelligence are more likely to be passed on to future generations.

BRAIN STRUCTURES

Different brain areas are associated with different types of mental processes and behaviors. For instance, the hippocampus is associated with short-term memory – the storage of information being thought about now.

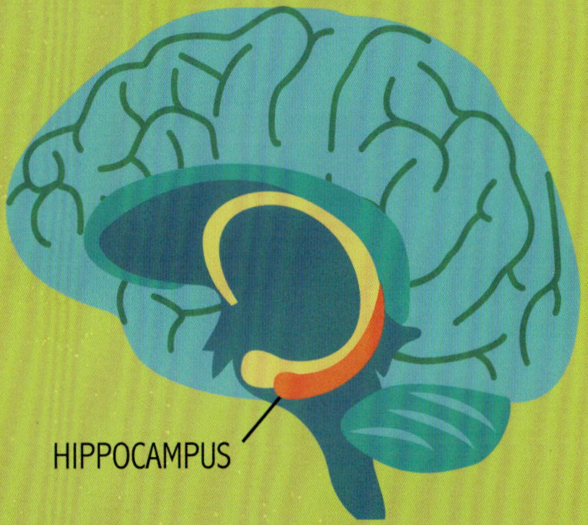

POSITIVE POINT

The biological approach uses physical measurements, such as brain scans, which helps psychologists study and analyze behavior.

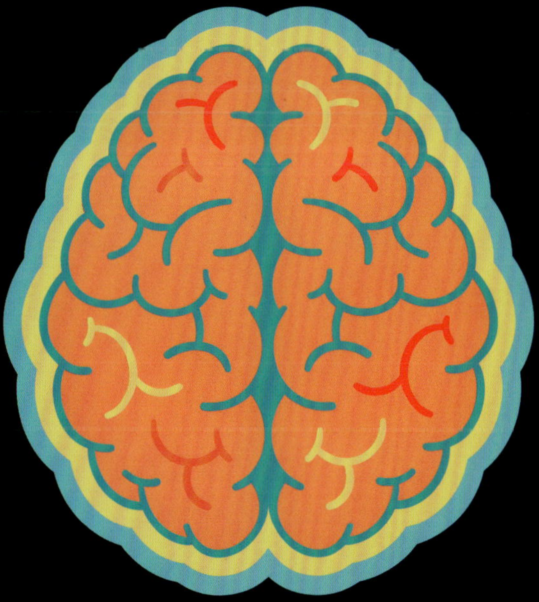

NEGATIVE POINT

The biological approach doesn't really consider how environmental learning experiences affect the mind and behavior.

Cynophobia (a fear of dogs) might be caused by a bad experience with dogs and not be an inherited characteristic.

A PRACTICAL APPLICATION

The biological approach has led to the development of drug treatments for mental disorders. For example, anti-psychotic drugs help people with schizophrenia.

THE COGNITIVE APPROACH: THE MIND AS A COMPUTER

The cognitive approach sees the mind working like a computer. There is an input of information (through the sensory organs: eyes, ears, nose, mouth, and skin) that is converted into electrical impulses and is sent via nerve fibers to the brain, which acts like a central processing unit in a computer to analyze the data.

The end product is an output, which in humans is not a print-out or display on a screen, but their behavior.

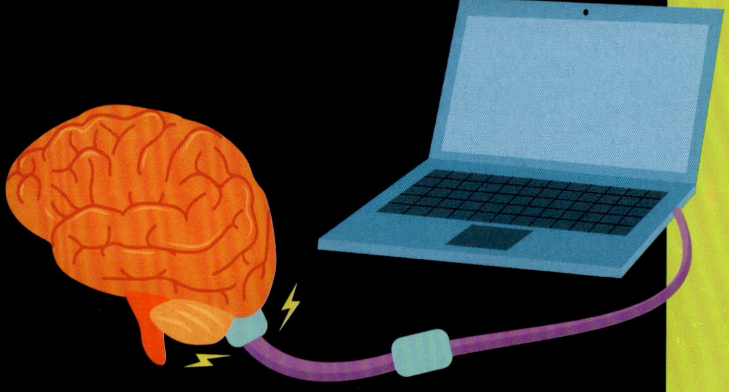

MENTAL PROCESSES

Cognitive psychologists study the mental processes that occur in the brain (like memory, thinking, and attention). It is these mental processes that are seen as motivating and controlling behavior.

SCHEMAS

Schemas concern our beliefs about the world (formed from our experiences of it). Schemas enable us to perceive and understand things in a pre-set way. To put it simply, we see what we expect to see based on previous experiences.

With Leeper's *Ambiguous Lady* (right) it is possible to see an old or a young lady. Young people's schemas generally prepare them to see the young woman in the illustration rather than the old woman. For older people the opposite can be true.

COGNITIVE NEUROSCIENCE

Cognitive neuroscience combines the biological and cognitive approaches by trying to identify which specific brain areas are involved with which specific mental processes.

For instance, research suggests that the fusiform gyrus brain area is involved in face recognition, allowing us to recognize familiar faces.

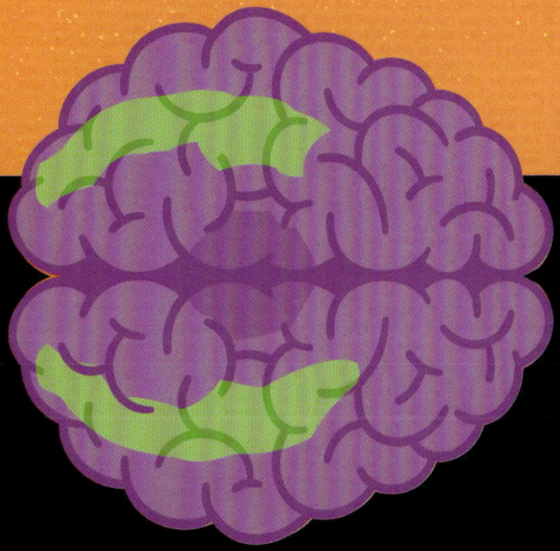

POSITIVE POINT

The cognitive approach sees behavior as resulting from the mental processes that occur between a stimuli and a response, and so can be considered superior to the behaviorist approach (see pages 10–11), which only sees behavior in terms of unthinking stimuli and responses.

NEGATIVE POINT

Seeing the mind as like a computer can make it seem a bit too machine-like. For instance, it ignores the important role that emotions play in motivating our behavior.

PRACTICAL APPLICATIONS

Findings from research into mental processes have led to helpful practical applications. For example, research into memory has led to study techniques to improve students' memories when preparing for exams.

THE BEHAVIORIST APPROACH: REFLEXES AND LEARNING

The behaviorist approach sees humans as *tabulae rasae* (blank slates), with all behavior learned from experience and no inherited genetic influences.

This approach only studies observable behavior (making it scientifically measurable), but this means there is no role for hidden mental processes, as with the cognitive approach (see pages 8–9). The approach often uses animal studies, as animals are seen as sharing principles of learning with humans.

Behaviorism focuses on three types of learning: **classical conditioning**, **social learning theory**, and **operant conditioning**.

CLASSICAL CONDITIONING

... involves reflex actions, where a response produced naturally by a specific stimulus becomes associated with another stimulus that is not normally associated with that response. This is done through experience, for example, learning to salivate to a bell. A dog will naturally salivate due to food, but not to a bell. But ring a bell at mealtimes enough times and eventually the dog will salivate just when the bell is rung.

BEFORE LEARNING
Food (UCS: unconditioned stimulus) =
Salivation (UCR: unconditioned response)

DURING LEARNING
Food (UCS) + Bell (CS: conditioned stimulus) =
Salivation (UCR)

AFTER LEARNING
Bell (CS) =
Salivation (CR: conditioned response)

SOCIAL LEARNING THEORY [SLT]

... involves learning through observation and imitation (copying) of role models whose behavior is seen to be vicariously reinforced (rewarded by others). We imitate the behavior if we believe that by doing so we will receive similar reinforcement.

This type of learning isn't strictly behaviorist, as it also involves using mental processes, like thinking and attention, before a behavior can be imitated.

OPERANT CONDITIONING

... involves voluntary behavior, with learning occurring through either **positive reinforcement**, where a behavior becomes likely to recur as it results in a pleasant outcome (being rewarded for cleaning your room results in you becoming more likely to clean your room in the future) or **negative reinforcement**, where a behavior becomes likely to recur as it avoids an unpleasant outcome (the threat of being grounded if you don't clean your room results in you being more likely to clean your room when needed).

POSITIVE POINT

This approach is supported by lots of scientific research that shows humans (and animals) do learn by using classical and operant conditioning and social learning theory. Our everyday experiences also show us that we learn in these ways.

NEGATIVE POINT

The approach only focuses on learning from experience and so ignores the important role biology plays, such as how genetics and evolution shape our behavior. Behaviorism also ignores the important role that mental processes play in determining behavior.

A PRACTICAL APPLICATION

This approach has led to successful treatments for mental disorders. Systematic desensitisation removes phobias, such as ophidophobia (fear of snakes), through the use of a step-by-step approach to a feared object or situation. A sufferer is taken through a series of steps using coping strategies that bring them closer and closer to a feared object or situation with each step.

THE PSYCHODYNAMIC APPROACH: THE UNCONSCIOUS MIND

The psychodynamic approach is associated with the work of Sigmund Freud (1856–1939) and sees **conscious behavior** influenced by the **unconscious mind**, which forms during childhood as you develop. The formation occurs through a system of biological drives and instincts motivating the development of your **personality**. Any unresolved traumas (crises) that occur during this development are **repressed** in the unconscious mind, and from there they can affect adult behavior.

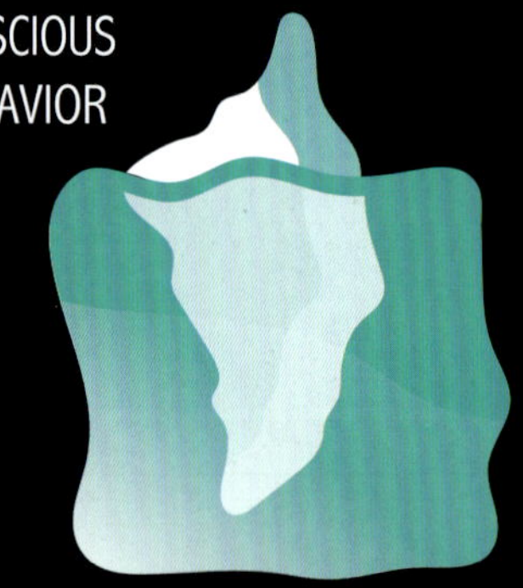

The vast unconscious mind exists "below the surface," so it cannot be seen – much like the largest part of an iceberg.

PSYCHOSEXUAL STAGES

Freud (left) argued that humans have a biological instinct to progress through what he called **psychosexual stages**. In each stage, psychic energy would be centered on a different part of the body. At the end of these stages of development, an adult personality would be fully formed.

THE DEVELOPMENT OF PERSONALITY

Freud saw personality as having three parts. Present from birth is the **id**, which is unrealistic, as it seeks selfish pleasure at all times. And then, from 18 months to 3 years of age, the **ego** develops, which has a more realistic view of things (for instance that pleasure can only be had at certain times). The ego seeks to provide a balance between the unrealistic demands of the id and the **super-ego**, which develops from 3 to 6 years of age and is again unrealistic, as it seeks for moral perfection at all times.

DEFENSE MECHANISMS

Anxiety reduces the ability of the ego to balance out the unrealistic demands of the id and super-ego. So defense mechanisms exist to reduce the effects of anxiety and thus keep the ego strong.

For instance, **repression** is a defense mechanism that hides unpleasant memories in the unconscious mind so they cannot make you anxious. They still, however, can affect conscious behavior. For instance, someone who has experienced abuse as a child may have problems forming adult relationships.

Repression makes us unaware of unpleasant memories so they cannot cause us anxiety.

POSITIVE POINT

The psychodynamic approach led to a general interest in psychology, leading to further research and greater understanding of thoughts and behavior.

NEGATIVE POINT

The psychodynamic approach relies a lot on evidence taken from case studies, which are in-depth studies of single individuals. Such evidence cannot really be generalized (said to be true for everyone).

A PRACTICAL APPLICATION

Psychotherapy is a form of mental health treatment that has developed from the psychodynamic approach. It works when psychoanalysts use various techniques (such as dream interpretation) to gain access to an individual's unconscious mind, so they can have insight into the source of their problems and learn to come to terms with them.

THE HUMANISTIC APPROACH: CONDITIONS OF WORTH

Humanism stresses holism, the idea that all aspects of a person should be considered collectively (together) in order to understand them, rather than examining individual parts of behavior on their own. Each individual's different experiences of life are seen as central to understanding who they are.

The approach sees individuals as being unique and possessing **free will** (having personal control over their thoughts and actions).

The approach also sees individuals as having an innate (inborn) drive to **self-actualize**.

SELF-ACTUALIZATION AND THE HIERARCHY OF NEEDS

When individuals achieve their full potential, they reach a state known as self-actualization (an ultimate feeling of well-being and satisfaction). Abraham Maslow (1908–1970) argued that this happens in a series of five stages, occurring in a set order, known as the **hierarchy of needs**. The needs of each stage must be met before you can progress onto the next stage and ultimately self-actualize.

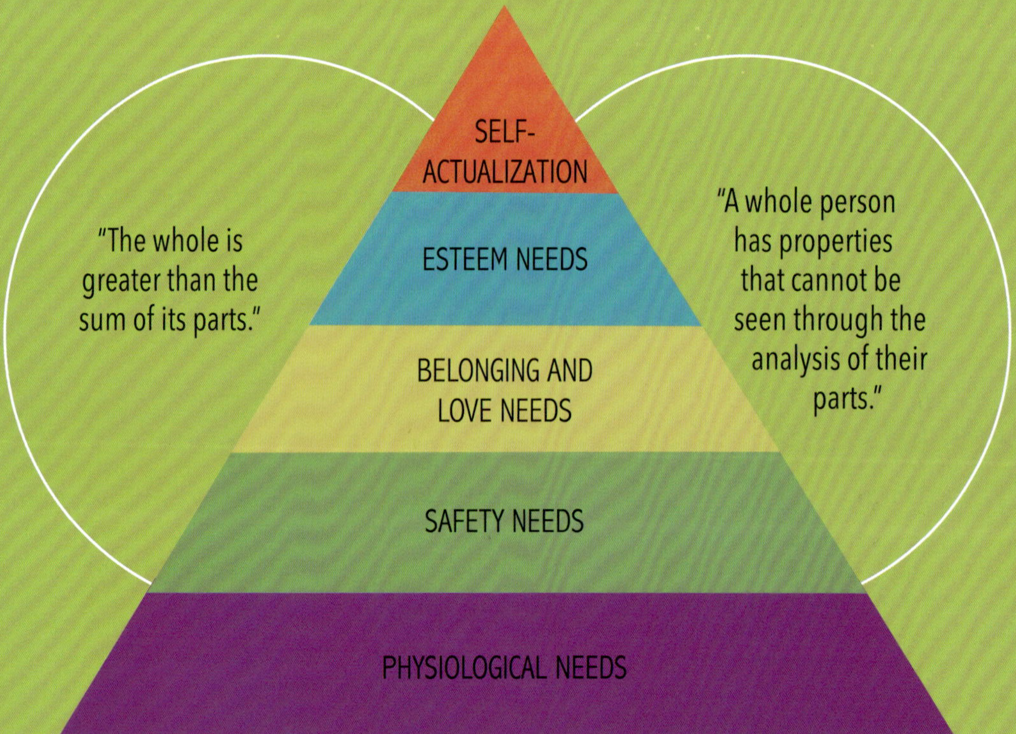

THE SELF

Carl Rogers (1902–1987) was a pioneer of humanist psychology, along with Maslow. He argued that humans have three selves:

1. **Self-image** – the way you see yourself.
2. **Ideal self** – the self you wish to be.
3. **Real self** – the self you actually are.

When the three selves are **congruent** (the same as each other) it becomes possible for individuals to self-actualize.

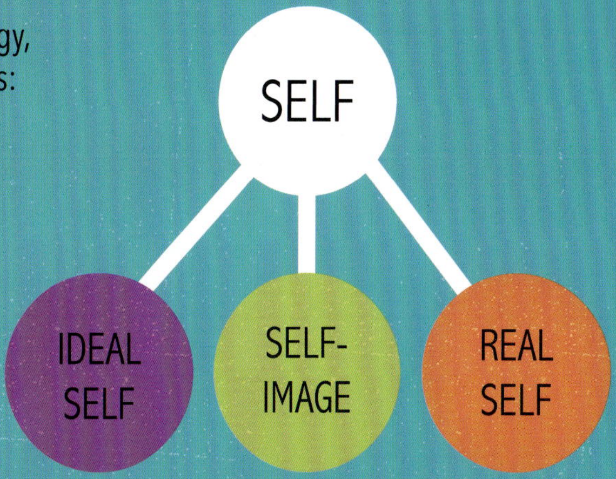

CONDITIONS OF WORTH

Rogers argued that achieving congruence of the self is only possible through having **unconditional positive regard** (being accepted totally by others for who you are). This requires **conditions of worth** – the requirements an individual feels they need in order to be loved.

Unconditional positive regard: accepting people as they are, instead of how you want them to be.

POSITIVE POINT

The approach sees individuals as being able to change for the better, and by doing so promotes self-growth and personal improvement.

NEGATIVE POINT

The approach neglects the important contribution of biology (for example, the role that genetics, biochemistry, and evolution play in determining behavior).

A PRACTICAL APPLICATION

Group counseling psychology is based on the humanistic approach, as seen through self-help groups, such as Alcoholics Anonymous. Members meet in an atmosphere of mutual acceptance and non-criticism to promote self-growth.

MORE PERSPECTIVES

Apart from the five main psychological approaches, this subject also embraces several other schools of thought. As well as each type contributing to an overall understanding of the mind and behavior, other types are also studied by themselves, often leading to beneficial practical applications. As can be seen, the types of psychology that make up the subject are very wide-ranging in their scope and interest.

SOCIAL PSYCHOLOGY

Social psychologists study how people's thoughts, feelings, and behavior are affected by others. The focus can be on how individuals affect other individuals or on group interactions, as humans are social animals, with much of their lives taking place via exchanges with other people. For example, social psychologists study obedience, looking at how and why people obey orders given by authority figures.

EVOLUTIONARY PSYCHOLOGY

Evolutionary psychology is a biological type of psychology that sees behaviors and characteristics that have a survival value as being genetically passed on and a result of natural selection. For example, having genes that dispose an individual to fear and avoid snakes could help them survive to adulthood (by not being bitten by poisonous snakes), and pass such "fear and avoid snake" genes on to their children. Over time, such genes would become more widespread throughout the population. This may explain why many people who fear snakes have never actually met one, let alone had a bad experience of one.

Evolutionary psychology can explain why individuals who have never had a bad experience of a snake might be afraid of them.

COGNITIVE NEUROSCIENCE

Cognitive neuroscience combines the biological and cognitive approaches to form a modern type of psychology that seeks to identify which particular brain structures are involved in specific types of cognitive processes. Cognitive neuroscience became possible with the advent of brain scanning techniques, such as magnetic resonance imaging (MRI), which have allowed the workings of the brain to be seen.

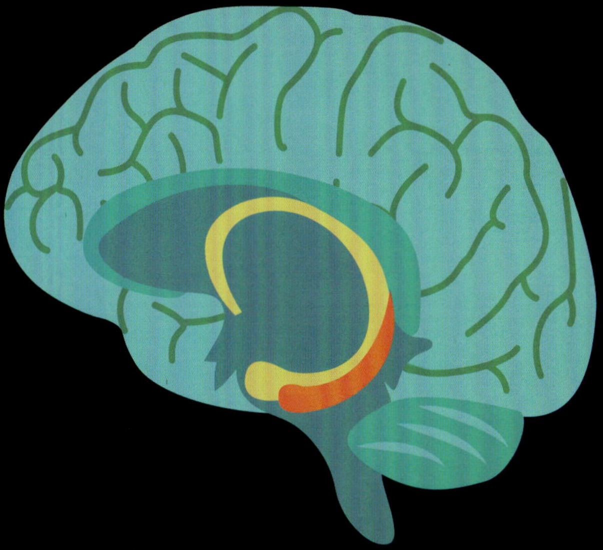

The brain is composed of many different parts and structures.

Developmental psychologists are especially interested in early childhood development, as much psychological growth occurs during this time.

DEVELOPMENTAL PSYCHOLOGY

Developmental psychologists study trends (changes over time) in human growth, with a focus upon physical, cognitive, social, and emotional development. Development in the early years is of particular interest but they study people of all ages, right through to senescence (old age), as development is a life-long process. Any developments that are universal (common to all) are seen as being under genetic control, while more individual developmental changes are seen as due to individual learning experiences.

EVEN MORE PERSPECTIVES

HEALTH PSYCHOLOGY

Health psychology focuses on how various psychological factors, including biological, cognitive, and social ones, affect people's health. There is a special focus on promoting healthy lifestyles and preventing illnesses. This is achieved through studying people's attitudes and behavioral responses to health and illness factors, as well as identifying how illnesses occur and methods to treat them. For example, health psychologists have identified a range of stress factors that can make people vulnerable to illness, and have devised effective strategies to deal with them.

Learning to see stress as a manageable challenge is one way in which health psychologists teach people to deal with stressors that could make them ill.

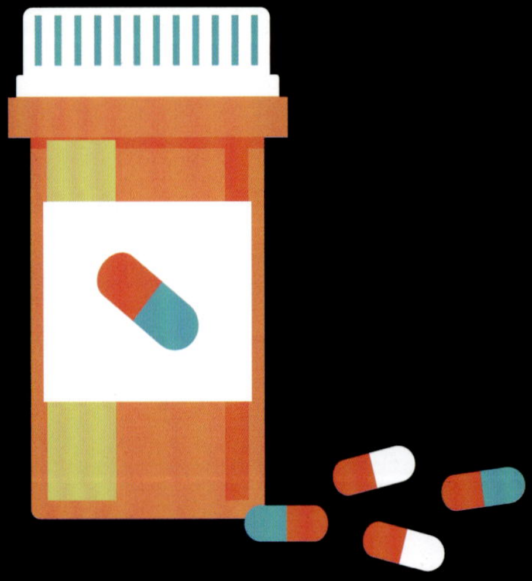

Anti-psychotic drugs are one way that clinical psychologists can treat schizophrenia.

CLINICAL PSYCHOLOGY

Clinical psychologists deal with mental disorders (from which 1 in 3 of us will suffer at least once during our lifetime), such as depression and anxiety disorders. They focus on creating accurate ways of diagnosing mental disorders and developing effective treatments. For example, a range of therapies have been developed to deal with schizophrenia, including anti-psychotic drugs – which have a direct biological effect to reduce symptoms – and cognitive behavioral therapy, which seeks to change the thought patterns of sufferers to alter their behavior and emotions.

FORENSIC PSYCHOLOGY

Forensic psychology deals with crime. It focuses on developing explanations of why people commit crimes and on developing strategies to reduce and prevent criminal behavior. For example, forensic psychologists have developed offender profiling systems, using psychology to identify likely criminal suspects, as well as developing means of dealing with criminals (other than just punishing them) so that they do not commit crimes again. This includes restorative justice programs, where offenders and the victims of their crimes meet in order to make offenders realize the negative impact their crimes have on others.

Anomalistic psychologists try to explain why some people want to believe that ghosts exist.

ANOMALISTIC PSYCHOLOGY

Anomalistic psychologists study paranormal experiences. They are not so much interested in whether things such as ghosts actually exist, but rather in why some people are compelled to believe such things exist. Anomalistic psychology has especially contributed to the development of unbiased and objective research methods, so that alleged paranormal experiences can be investigated without risk of trickery and manipulation occurring. For example, psychologists now understand how "cold reading" works, where fake psychics use techniques, such as analyzing an individual's body language, to make fairly accurate guesses about their beliefs and behavior.

ANIMAL PSYCHOLOGY

Animal psychologists study the physiological and psychological functioning of animals as a way to better understand humans, but also as a means of studying animal species themselves. Such knowledge is becoming especially important in helping to conserve endangered animal species. For example, imprinting, a technique where some bird species follow the first moving object they encounter, has been used to imprint whooping crane chicks onto a micro-light aircraft, which then shows them the migration paths to winter feeding grounds.

Animal psychologists have used imprinting to help endangered migratory birds.

PRACTICAL APPLICATIONS: THE BENEFITS OF PSYCHOLOGY

As with other sciences, psychology, through conducting research and establishing theories, has provided practical applications of value to individuals and society as a whole. Not only have such applications improved people's health and well-being, they also benefit the economy. For example, developing effective mental health therapies means that fewer people need expensive mental health care and are able to work and earn money. The practical applications generated by psychology are very wide-ranging.

Practical applications based on psychological research and theories not only improve well-being, they also benefit the economy.

MENTAL HEALTH THERAPIES

Psychologists have developed effective treatments for many mental health disorders. Drug therapies are cost-effective and can either be given by themselves or in combination with other therapies. Such psychological therapies include cognitive therapies, where irrational thought processes are replaced with more rational (sensible) ones; behavioral therapies, where problematic behavior is eradicated by reinforcing (rewarding) more desirable behavior; and humanistic counseling therapies, where individuals discuss their problems without criticism in order to improve their self-esteem.

Psychological therapies have proven effective in treating a wide range of mental disorders.

SPORTS PSYCHOLOGY

Sports psychologists not only use psychology to improve the performances of athletes and teams, they also make recommendations concerning which activities are suitable for different types of people. For example, there is no point trying to teach very young children games requiring interaction between players, as such children are egocentric – they would not understand that playing football effectively involves passing the ball to other players!

Most elite athletes and teams employ sports psychologists in order to maximize their performance. They are considered to be as important as coaches, physical therapists, and nutritionists are.

Relationship counseling can help people who are experiencing problems with romantic relationships.

RELATIONSHIP COUNSELING

Over 40 percent of marriages end in divorce, and this can cause long-term harm, emotionally, socially, and financially, to individuals and their families. Psychology provides an effective practical application in relationship counseling, which helps couples solve their problems and save their relationships, or break up in a way that reduces such forms of harm.

OTHER USES

There are many other uses for psychology for both individuals and society.

Educational psychology uses research to design suitable educational programs for children of different ages.

Industrial psychologists help to reduce stress in the workplace by devising work practices that reduce worker stress and increase worker satisfaction, which reduces the amount of people that have to take time off due to stress and thus increases productivity.

Agricultural psychologists carry out research on farm animals to develop ways of improving their well-being that benefits the animals themselves, as well as helping farmers in terms of improved profits. This has included altering cow herd sizes to increase the amount of milk they produce, and playing music to pigs!

Research shows that pigs grow bigger when played classical music.

HOW PSYCHOLOGISTS CONDUCT RESEARCH

Because psychology is a science, psychologists conduct scientific experiments as their main method of research. However, in situations where experiments wouldn't be suitable, non-scientific methods of research are used instead. Different research methods are used to suit different circumstances.

Which research method is used depends on what specifically is being searched for.

THE EXPERIMENTAL METHOD

Researchers need to make sure experiments are conducted under controlled conditions. This means everything is the same throughout an experiment, except the independent variable (IV).

For example, if you were testing the physical effects of sleep by giving participants either eight hours of sleep or no sleep and then measuring their reaction times (the dependent variable, or DV), sleep time would be the IV. All other variables must be kept the same for all participants. In this way causality (cause and effect relationships) can be seen.

TYPES OF EXPERIMENTS

Psychologists use four basic experiments:

1. **Laboratory experiments**
   Conducted under controlled conditions.
2. **Field experiments**
   Conducted in real-world settings (which means controlled conditions are harder to achieve).
3. **Quasi experiments**
   Use a naturally-occurring independent variable that is not manipulated by researchers (such as gender or ethnic background).
4. **Natural experiments**
   Use an independent variable that varies naturally and so is not manipulated by the researchers.

A field experiment could be used to see if we are more likely to obey individuals in uniform in real-world situations.

NON-EXPERIMENTAL (ALTERNATIVE) METHODS

1 Correlational studies
Assess the degree of relationship between co-variables, for example the number of hours spent studying and the score on a test. These studies are often used when an experiment would be unethical, such as when assessing the relationship between smoking and cancer.

2 Observational studies
Involve recording naturally occurring behavior in real-world situations. Often used in situations where conducting an experiment wouldn't be practical, such as studying the behavior of sports fans.

3 Case studies
Involve in-depth, detailed investigation of one person or a small group of people. Often used to study unique or rare individuals, such as children raised by animals.

4 Self-reports
Involve participants giving information about themselves, usually either via interview or questionnaire.

As non-experimental research methods are not generally conducted under controlled conditions, causality is harder to establish and replication is also harder to achieve to check results.

THE IMPORTANCE OF RESEARCH METHODS

Psychologists generate **theories** – educated guesses – from research. They use the theories to create practical applications – ways of using psychology in the real world. However, if the theories are wrong, then the practical applications based on them can be flawed and cause harm. Therefore, for practical applications to be of value, the theories from which they are formed must be based upon strong research. As a result, it can be said that research methods are the most important component of psychology.

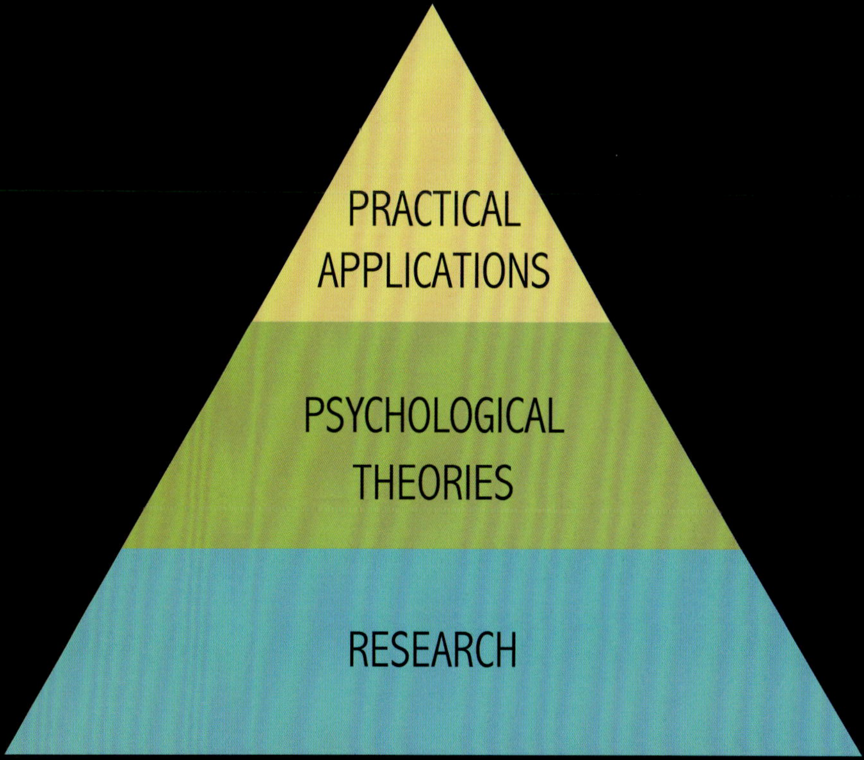

Properly designed and conducted research is the foundation upon which psychological theories and practical applications are based.

BIG ISSUES AND DEBATES

Psychology has its origins in philosophy. Therefore, contained within the psychological approaches and research methods are many philosophical debates and issues. These are not easily resolved, but, instead, should be seen as differing points of view, with each viewpoint having its strengths and weaknesses.

Let's take a look at some of the main issues and debates that psychology concerns itself with.

FREE WILL VS. DETERMINISM

Free will sees individuals having conscious control over thoughts and actions, while determinism sees thoughts and behavior resulting from forces beyond conscious control. We evidently have some free will. For example, no one can make you stand up just by telling you to if you don't want to. But you probably don't have as much free will as you think you have, as evolutionary forces, which through natural selection shape the genes you possess, influence your behavior.

The biological and behaviorist approaches are both determinist, as they see behavior as being either determined by biology or by learning experiences, with little, if any, room for free will. The humanist approach, though, sees humans as having total free will over their thoughts and actions with no role for determinism.

How much are our thoughts and behaviors controlled by external sources?

THE NATURE VS. NURTURE DEBATE

The nature side of the debate sees behavior and mental abilities as innate rather than learned, which fits the biological approach. The nurture side of the debate takes the opposite viewpoint, seeing behavior and mental abilities as learned from environmental experiences, which fits the behaviorist approach. Studies of twins favor the nature viewpoint if identical twins (100 percent genetically similar) are more similar in behavior than non-identical twins.

More favored nowadays is the interactionist viewpoint, which sees individuals as having different genetic potential for behaviors and abilities – for example, level of intelligence – with environmental factors, such as levels of stress, determining how much of your genetic potential is realized.

HOLISM VS. REDUCTIONISM

Holism argues that the best way to understand a behavior is to view it in its entirety (as a whole) rather than it being the sum of its parts. Reductionism takes the opposite stance – that a behavior is best understood by breaking it down to its basic parts and studying these in isolation from each other.

An attempt to resolve this debate concerns levels of explanation, which focuses on what type of explanation is required. If a reductionist explanation of aggression was needed, then a biological approach might be taken, like understanding aggression in terms of genes and biochemistry (for instance specific genes and levels of testosterone). However, if a more holistic explanation is required, the focus might be on learning experiences, mental processes, and social factors, like family influences, that influence an individual's level of aggression.

Is an individual best understood as a whole person or as the sum of their parts?

INFORMED CONSENT

Researchers should give potential participants and/or participants' parents sufficient details of a study so that they can make an educated decision as to whether they wish to take part.

RIGHT TO WITHDRAW

Participants should be informed, before a study commences, that they are under no obligation to take part and that they can withdraw (leave) at any time they wish. This includes withdrawing data after a study has finished.

ETHICAL ISSUES

The advancement of psychology is dependent upon people (and animals) participating in research. But research must be conducted in an ethical manner that protects the health and dignity of participants and the reputation of the subject. If unethical research was allowed, then psychologists would not be respected and people would be reluctant to participate in research studies. Therefore a code of ethics has been drawn up that psychologists must follow when designing and conducting research. The code includes the following areas:

AVOIDANCE OF DECEPTION

Researchers should not withhold information about a study from participants (for example the purpose for which it is being conducted) or give misleading information to participants.

PROTECTION FROM HARM

Researchers have a responsibility to protect their participants from physical and mental harm during an investigation. The risk of harm should be no greater than participants would face in their everyday lives. Ideally participants should leave a study in the same physical and mental state that they entered it.

CONFIDENTIALITY/ANONYMITY

Researchers should not disclose participants' data to anyone, unless it was agreed in advance. Confidentiality means that data can be traced back to names, whereas, with anonymity, data cannot, as researchers do not collect participants' names.

OBSERVATIONAL RESEARCH

Observational studies generally take place in real-life situations. When conducting such research, observations should occur in public places where people would expect to be observed by strangers.

ADEQUATE BRIEFING/DEBRIEFING

All relevant details of a study should be explained to a participant beforehand (briefing) and afterward (debriefing).

ANIMAL RESEARCH

Ethical guidelines for those conducting research upon wild animals in their natural habitat state that studies should be conducted in ways that do not endanger their well-being.

Ethical guidelines that relate to laboratory-based research upon captive animals revolve mainly around the conditions that the animals are kept in, such as giving them access to food and water. This has led to controversy around the degree of harm that should be permitted to animals participating in research. Some argue that the means (harm to animals) is justified by the ends (increased knowledge/creation of beneficial practical applications), while others argue that such harm is never justifiable.

INCENTIVES TO PARTICIPATE

Participants should take part in a study because they want to, not because they are pressured to do so. Therefore, they should not be promised rewards, such as money or gifts, for participating, as this may pressure them to take part against their will.

IMPORTANT STUDIES

Thousands of psychological studies of varying types are carried out every year, each contributing to our understanding of the mind and behavior. On our final stop of this tour of psychology, let's have a look at a few studies that have made important contributions.

ROBERT WILLIAMS'S TEST (1972)

IQ tests claimed to assess innate intelligence, not learned knowledge. Such tests regularly showed white people, on average, scored 15 IQ points higher than Black people, supporting the claim that white people were naturally smarter than Black people.

However, with his Black Intelligence Test for Cultural Homogeneity, Robert Williams (1930–2020) showed that what IQ tests actually test was learned cultural knowledge, not natural levels of intelligence. His test was based on Black American cultural knowledge, with Black participants (average score 87/100) easily outscoring white participants on the test (average score 51/100). These findings showed that standard IQ tests, often used as selection tests for jobs and schools, were biased against non-white individuals.

Williams's study showed how standard IQ tests were racially biased against Black people

FALSE MEMORIES OF BUGS BUNNY: ELIZABETH LOFTUS AND JACQUELINE PICKRELL [2003]

Elizabeth Loftus and Jacqueline Pickrell conducted a study that created false memories in adult participants who had visited Disneyland as children. Participants had to read some information about Disneyland and answer questions about their childhood memories of it. If Bugs Bunny was mentioned in the information and/or a cardboard cutout of Bugs Bunny was present in the laboratory, participants tended to recall meeting Bugs Bunny at Disneyland. This was impossible as Bugs Bunny is a Warner Bros. character. The researchers had shown that recall of events is not necessarily true, especially if false information is suggested to someone after an event has occurred.

OBEDIENCE TO AUTHORITY: STANLEY MILGRAM (1963)

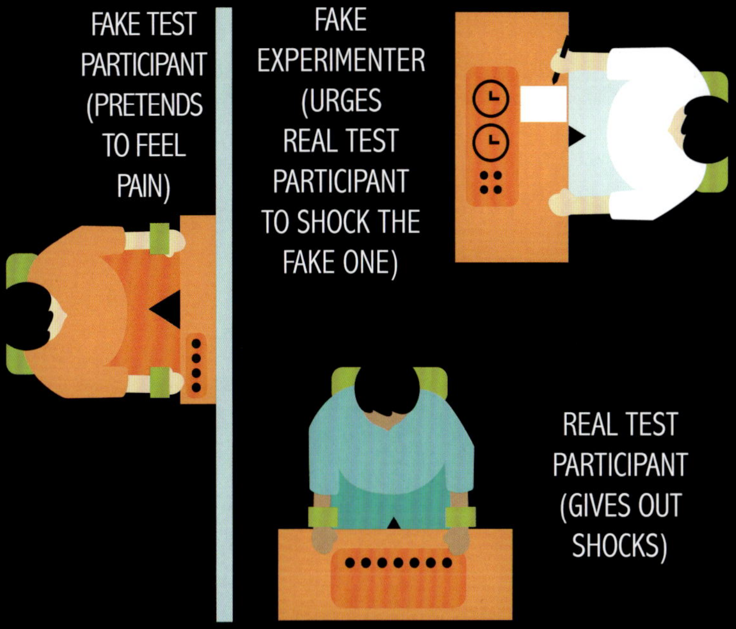

The layout of Milgram's study into obedience to authority is shown here.

Prompted by the obedience shown by many German people to the destructive orders of the Nazis during World War II (1939–1945), Stanley Milgram (1933–1984) got participants to give increasing levels of electric shocks (which weren't actually real) to someone who answered questions incorrectly, merely because an authority figure – a man wearing a lab coat – told them to. More than 60 percent of participants gave the potentially lethal maximum voltage of 450 volts when told.

Participants were distressed by their behavior; many cried and argued with the authority figure, and three of them had seizures. But they obeyed, showing that people will obey authority figures even when it goes against their moral code.

VISUAL CLIFF: ELEANOR GIBSON AND RICHARD WALK (1960)

Newly married psychologists Eleanor Gibson (1910–2002) and Richard Walk (1920–1999) had an argument at a picnic by the Grand Canyon. Gibson feared their young children would crawl over the edge and fall to their deaths. Walk argued they had a natural ability to perceive depth and thus wouldn't crawl over the edge.

They took the argument into the laboratory, devising a testing device called the **visual cliff**. A baby was placed on one side of the device with its mother calling to it from the other side. To get to its mother, the baby would have to crawl over an apparent vertical drop (they were protected from doing so by a sheet of glass that they couldn't see). Babies refused to cross the apparent drop, proving Walk's theory that depth perception is largely innate.

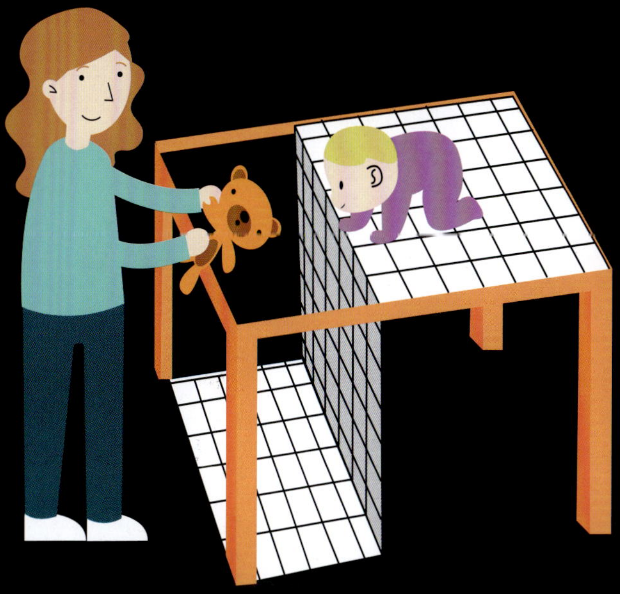

The Visual Cliff assesses whether infants have an innate sense of depth perception.

GLOSSARY

abuse
Cruel, unfair or violent treatment

ambiguous
Something that can be understood in more than one way

anti-psychotic
Acting against psychosis, which means feeling out of touch with reality, a feature of some mental illnesses

anxiety disorder
Excessive and uncontrollable fear or anxiety in response to situations

behaviorism
The theory that human behavior is the result of conditioning, and not the result of thoughts and feelings

biochemistry
The study of the structure of living things

biological
Connected to biology, the study of the life and structure of plants and animals

characteristic
A feature or quality of someone's personality or body type

cognitive
Connected to the process of understanding and learning

cognitive behavioral therapy
A type of therapy where the therapist encourages the client to challenge and change negative ways of thinking and behaving in order to help the person understand themselves and the world around them and change patterns of behavior

conditioning
Changing behavior in a person or animal by weakening the link between the stimulus and the response

congruent
Similar to something and not in conflict with it

DNA (deoxyribonucleic acid)
The material that carries genetic information, found in every cell in your body

depression
A mental illness in which someone feels very sad and hopeless for a long time

environmental learning
The idea that a person's environment shapes their learning and behavior

evolution
The process of change over time that occurs due to natural selection, where positive characteristics are more likely to survive and be passed down to future generations

gene
One of the many instructions carried in our cells, which tells our body how to work

hierarchy
A system where people or things are organized into different levels

hormone
A substance that is produced by a gland in the body and released into the blood, where it affects the workings of cells and tissues in the body

humanistic approach
The idea that you should study the whole person rather than focusing on particular behaviors

inherited characteristic
Any of thousands of characteristics that are passed down to offspring from their biological parents

instinct
A behavior that is not learned or practiced but occurs naturally in people or a species of animal

motivate
To make someone behave a certain way

natural selection
The theory, originally proposed by Charles Darwin, that individuals with the most favorable characteristics are more likely to survive and have offspring

neuroscience
The study of the brain and nervous system

neurotransmitter
A chemical that crosses the tiny gap between one neuron (nerve cell or brain cell) and another, passing the electrical signal from the brain on to the next part of the nervous system

personality
The different parts of your character that make you different from the next person

phobia
A strong, unreasonable fear of something

potential
In terms of people, the qualities or abilities that could be developed or used

principle
A general truth or belief

productivity
The rate at which a worker, organization, or country produces goods, as compared to the amount of time they spend doing it

psychodynamic approach
The theory that people's behavior is caused by the conscious and unconscious mind

psychological factors
Elements affecting the way people act, including thoughts, feelings, understanding, attitudes, and personality traits

reflex
Something that you do without thinking

repression
Controlling strong feelings or thoughts so much that others are not aware of them and they seem not to exist

role model
Someone you look up to or admire and try to copy

schema
A plan, a belief, or a set of information that helps us interpret information and understand things in a pre-set way, based on previous experience

schizophrenia
A mental illness that causes someone to withdraw from reality

self-actualization
Being able to reach your potential – developing your own abilities

self-esteem
Feeling content with your own character and skills

stimuli
Things that produce a reaction in a human or animal

strategy
A plan of action

systematic desensitisation
A treatment for fears or phobias where, step-by-step, someone is exposed to the thing that they are afraid of, to help them overcome the fear

testosterone
The male sex hormone. During puberty, this hormone causes men to develop the characteristics of the male body

unconscious mind
The part of your mind that you're unaware of

FURTHER INFORMATION

BOOKS

The Bright and Bold Human Body: The Brain and Nervious System (Wayland, 2019)

The Psyschology Book (DK, 2012)

Your Mind Matters (series, Franklin Watts, 2019)

WEBSITES

kids.britannica.com/kids/article/psychology/353676
This website has lots of information on psychology and related topics.

www.mind.org.uk/information-support/for-children-and-young-people
The website of MIND, a charity that offers support and advice for people struggling with mental health, helps to explain mental health problems to all.

INDEX